M Y T H

PERSONAL IDEALISM

M Y T H E O L O G Y

KEITH WARD

PERSONAL
IDEALISM

DARTON·LONGMAN+TODD

First published in 2021 by
Darton, Longman and Todd Ltd
1 Spencer Court
140 – 142 Wandsworth High Street
London SW18 4JJ

© 2021 Keith Ward

The right of Keith Ward to be identified as the Author of this work has been asserted in accordance with the Copyright, Designs and Patents Act 1988.

ISBN: 978-1-913657-58-1

A catalogue record for this book is available from the British Library.

Printed and bound in Great Britain by
Bell & Bain, Glasgow

Contents

Introduction		7
1.	The Existence of God	13
2.	Good and Evil	23
3.	The Philosophy of Idealism	29
4.	Revelation	37
5.	Interpreting the Bible	45
6.	The Kingdom of God	55
7.	The World to Come	61
8.	The Incarnation	69
9.	The Atonement	79
10.	The Trinity and the Redemption of the Cosmos	85
Appendix		95

From my earliest years I have been interested in the big questions about human life – does life have any meaning? Does it have any purpose? Is there some way in which humans ought to live? Is consciousness really just a complex arrangement of material particles in the brain? Is freedom of choice an illusion? Is human life all just some sort of cosmic accident? At first my parents just thought I was rather odd, but at University I discovered there was a subject where these questions were taken seriously. This was philosophy, so I studied it, and, amazingly, I got jobs teaching philosophy at various British and American Universities.

Religions often deal with these questions, so I was interested in them, too, and I moved gradually into philosophy of religion, and then into theology, ending my main academic career as the Regius Professor of Divinity at the

University of Oxford, and becoming a Fellow of the British Academy.

My views varied a great deal in my early years. Sometimes I was an atheist – religions said so many conflicting things. Sometimes I was attracted to some faith – I particularly liked Vedantic Hinduism (the 'perennial philosophy') and some versions of Christianity. As a philosopher I stood in the 'Oxford' tradition of linguistic analysis, but was also heavily influenced by Wittgenstein, by Kant, and by the British Empiricists Locke, Berkeley, and Hume. I took a very wide and eclectic view of religions, but I was always attracted to life-enhancing and universally compassionate views rather than more guilt-ridden and exclusive ones.

Then, at a certain stage, as an adult, I had a strong personal experience of the presence of Jesus Christ, so I was baptised and confirmed in the Church in Wales. Some years later I was ordained as a priest, while I was teaching philosophy at King's College, London. Since then, I have always worked as an honorary

INTRODUCTION

curate in the nearest available church, and in that half of my life I ended up as at one time Dean of Trinity Hall, Cambridge, and later as a Canon of Christ Church, Oxford.

This double career accounts for how my theological views developed. My interest in mathematical physics, nurtured by John Polkinghorne and Arthur Peacocke in Cambridge, and in the philosophy of Kant, led to my becoming a personal Idealist (briefly explained later in this book). Most traditional Christian theology has used Plato or Aristotle as a background to theology. If things are to be formulated in personal Idealist terms, this will have to change – though the influence of the ancient Greek philosophers will never fade.

My interest in world religions led to my adopting a very non-exclusive view of Christian faith. As an Anglican, both Catholic and Protestant strands lie in my tradition, though a form of liberal Protestantism is most common among Idealists. To them I have added various Indian and Enlightenment influences. This produces a theology every item of which will be denied by some Christians, but which, taken as a whole, I hope will suggest a spirituality which is both centred on Christ and is consonant with the best contemporary knowledge of the world.

1
The Existence of God

HAVING BEEN AN atheist, I know that if there is no God, there is no reason to take Jesus seriously, since he was mistaken about some of the most important questions of life. So one big question to address is whether there is a God, and we have to ask first what we mean by God, what God is like.

God in Jewish, Muslim, and Christian traditions, is taken to have supreme knowledge, supreme creative power, and supreme goodness. If such a being created anything, it would create things for the sake of their intrinsic goodness or value. An intrinsic value is something that is worth existing just for its own sake. For instance, if you ask, 'Why aim at happiness?', the only obvious answer is, 'Because it is good'. There is a good reason for any conscious being to choose it. It is not good as a means to something else; it is intrinsically good; it is reasonable to choose it just for its own sake.

Other intrinsic values are states such as: knowledge, understanding, creativity (ability to do new things), the appreciation of beauty, and friendship (which includes co-operation and compassion). These are states which are intrinsically good, they are worth-while goals or purposes for any conscious, feeling, choosing (intelligent) being.

I think that a supreme mind (God) would choose for itself the highest degree of such intrinsic values which could co-exist. If friendship is a great intrinsic good, it will create other minds to which it can relate.

This means that the cosmos will have what is called a personal explanation. This explains why something is as it is because it is intrinsically good, and is chosen by a conscious being for that reason. Personal explanation, in terms of purposes and values, is quite different from scientific explanation, which is in terms of initial physical states and predictable laws, without reference to purposes and values at all. It looks as though if we want to explain our world, personal explanation must be added to scientific explanation. In fact, scientific explanation cannot account for purposes and values, whereas personal explanation is a good explanation of why the initial physical states and laws are what they are – because they seem to be exactly what is required to make the specific intrinsic goods of this universe possible.

If some ultimate mind, which knows all possibilities, knows which are good, acts to realise some good states, and enjoys them, that would be a completely satisfactory explanation of why the cosmos exists. That is the hypothesis of God.

Some people think that a supreme mind could not exist without a brain. But I know that I have thoughts and feelings before I learn that they are connected, in an admittedly mysterious way, to my brain. As the philosopher David Hume said, what I can without contradiction conceive apart could logically exist apart. I cannot see any contradiction in the existence of thoughts and even perceptions existing without any physical body or brain. There may be a deeply hidden contradiction, but if we cannot find one, we have to remain open to the possibility that non-embodied minds could exist. God cannot be ruled out just by definition.

But, some people ask, if we explain the universe by saying that some Mind created it, what created that Mind? God, the supreme Mind, created time, so is not in time (God is timeless). If God is timeless, God cannot be brought into being, for then there would be a time when God was not, followed by a time when God was. That is impossible. It follows that the question, 'What created God?' is a nonsensical question. It asks, 'Who brought into being something which is incapable of being brought into being?' And this is nonsense. Ultimate Mind is eternal, and cannot be caused or destroyed.

If an eternal Mind created the cosmos, it made something which was always possible into something actual, and it did so for a purpose, in order to create good states. That is what minds do, when they are working properly. Possibilities cannot just exist on their own, because possible things do not actually exist. If there really are possibilities, they must exist in something that is actual. The obvious place where possible things exist is in minds. Even in our minds, we can think of many possible things. Eternal Mind thinks of every possible thing. So, this Mind is maximally knowing.

Some people say that God is omnipotent and omniscient. I do not object to that, but if so, omnipotence cannot mean that God can do absolutely anything, and omniscience cannot mean that God knows absolutely everything, past, present and future. That would lead to logical problems, but they are easily avoided. God cannot do anything that contradicts God's own nature. God cannot, for instance, do something evil, or commit suicide, or turn into a frog. But God can still be maximally powerful – more powerful than any other being, actual or possible.

God is also a personal being who co-operates with and responds to finite beings who are free and temporal. For God realises in the divine being all perfections, and they will include the creative ability to do new things and the capacity for friendship and love. If God is creative and responsive in such ways, God must be capable of change, and so in some sense temporal (but not confined to our spacetime, of course). I have said that God is eternal, but the more complex fact is that God is eternal and changeless in some respects and free and changing in others. There is no problem in this; for instance, one can be necessarily loving, but changing in the ways of expressing that love. God can exist, be maximally creative, knowing, and loving, all eternally and changelessly, yet there may be many changing ways in which God expresses creativity, and many things that God has not decided yet. Even God cannot know what those are. There are some states which even a maximally knowing and maximally creative being cannot know. God is still, however, maximally knowing, knowing more than any other actual or possible being.

Another important property of God is that if all possible worlds exist in the mind of God (as possibilities), then God must exist by necessity. If there is any possible world, God must exist as that in which the possible world exists, and without God no possible worlds could exist. To put it in logical terms, God exists in every possible world, which is one definition of a necessarily existing being.

Some philosophers have said that there cannot be a necessarily existing being. I can always imagine a world without God. All existence is contingent – it might not have existed, and that, it is said, goes for God too. But this is mistaken. You might think you can imagine a world without God. But you have not really imagined a world in all its complexity and all the conditions of its existence. Possible worlds cannot exist except in something actual, which is the mind of God. God is a necessary condition of there being any world. Since this world, and perhaps many worlds, were always possible, God is uncreated and eternal Mind, maximally knowing and creative, existing by necessity, creator of everything other than itself, and capable of new creative actions and responsive relationships to creatures.

2
Good and Evil

GOD WILL ALSO be good, for God will desire that what is created is worth-while, good just for its own sake. There is a complication here, for there is much evil and suffering in the world. At this point, it is important to remember that many features of the divine nature are necessarily what they are; even God cannot change them. The mystery of suffering is hidden in these necessities of the divine nature. We obviously do not know in anything like a complete way what such necessities are. But we know that humans are microcosms of the universe. In a way, we recapitulate in the womb the history of the cosmos, from bare molecular structure through forms of increasingly complex organic life to consciousness and intelligence. This strongly suggests that we could only be the carbon-based creative, relational, emergent, and partly autonomous life-forms we are in a universe like this – and, cosmologists tell us, precisely like this. Even if God did not have to create exactly this universe, perhaps God necessarily creates a universe which contains intelligent beings of the same general sort as us, and so is subject to some constraints, inherent in the necessary divine nature.

Modern cosmology suggests that God created an unconscious value-neutral formless void (like the 'formless deep' of Genesis 1:1). From this primal void, complex structures and integrated forms developed in a long emergent process toward conscious intelligence. It is reasonable to view this process as directed towards intelligent life, not as pure random change without any purpose or value. The process moves towards value, but it is an emergent process of multiple and partly self-directing entities, governed by general laws which are rational and intelligible, but which also allow for a number of alternative futures which created entities may follow. In the early stages of cosmic evolution, this permits elements of seeming randomness in the way things go. At later stages such randomness is progressively replaced by conscious choices, and these may be, and in the human case often are, conflictual and egoistic choices which frustrate the divine purpose. God's purpose remains good, and, Christians believe, will ultimately prevail. But God leaves the creative autonomy of the world intact, and thus the way to goodness is often difficult and even seemingly frustrated. The death of Jesus, which seemed to frustrate his mission, is the key Christian symbol of this, and that death of course ultimately led to good.

The cosmos is an emergent and autonomous and yet estranged reality; so, while God is necessarily good, and wills good for the world, God must realise such goodness within the constraints of the inner necessities of being. Even a maximally powerful, knowing, and good being is limited by the necessities of its own nature. There is no alternative.

3
The Philosophy of Idealism

THAT, IN MY view, is what God is like. But does God exist? I want to stress that this is a deep philosophical question, and that the answer lies in some fundamental philosophical commitments. Philosophers differ about these things, but all would agree that what is at stake is what reality is ultimately like. Believing in God is not accepting some sort of optional addition to a universe we all agree about, but expresses a rational reflection on the nature of ultimate reality.

In modern philosophy, materialism, sometimes called 'naturalism', is a widely held philosophy. It is the view that everything that exists is made of matter located in spacetime, or, in a weaker form, that mental events like perceptions, thoughts, and feelings could not exist without a material basis. Opposed to this view is the philosophy of Idealism, which is the view that everything that exists is consciousness or mind or, in a weaker form, that material things could not exist without a mental basis. All believers in God are Idealists, though most are weak Idealists.

The Idealist view seems to me to be the right one. The reason for this is that all knowledge begins with experience. The first step towards Idealism is to see that without sense-perceptions (awareness of colours, smells, tastes, and touches) we would have no knowledge at all. Without feelings, we could not distinguish between good and bad experiences. Without thoughts, we could not make sense of our perceptions by thinking of them as perceptions of external objects. Without intentions, we could not actively explore and understand our environment. Sense-perceptions, thoughts, feelings, and intentions undeniably exist. They are the first things we know, and the things we are most sure of. We might not know whether what we see is an illusion or a dream, but at least we know that we are having visual sensations

THE PHILOSOPHY OF IDEALISM

and making decisions. Such sensations and intentions exist; they are parts of the furniture of the universe.

The second step towards Idealism is to see that perceptions, thoughts and feelings are not the same as or reducible to material qualities such as mass, spatial location, gravitational attraction or electric charge. In modern physics, colours like green or tastes like sweetness are not properties which exist apart from our perception of them. I see a green patch; it exists. But a physicist will point out that what is happening is that a certain wavelength of light hits the retina, and is turned into electrical signals to various parts of the brain, which then generate the sensation of greenness. The sensation is very different from the objective wavelength. The same sort of thing is true of all our perceptions. What we perceive (coloured solid three-dimensional objects) does not exist when it is not being observed. Without observations the physical properties of the world, according to physics, are entities like force-fields or probabilistic wave-forms, perhaps in eleven dimensions, which we never perceive as they are. If so, the world we perceive is a function of our consciousness, not what exists in an unobserved physical world.

The idea of the physical world which physics, especially quantum physics, gives, is very different from the world of perceptions, thoughts, feelings, values, and purposes. The third step towards Idealism is to see that there are not two quite different worlds, one of physical particles and another of mental states, connected in a mysterious way. Instead, conscious experience is the fundamental reality. The world of physics is an abstract conception of those parts of our consciously perceived world that can be mathematically described and predicted. In other words, minds and their contents are more real than the supposed 'objective' physical world of unobserved objects, which is a sort of mathematical construction that we postulate to make sense of our experience.

Of course, there is an external reality

which gives rise to our experiences. But that reality too is composed of consciousness. In my opinion it is a divine mind which creates ('thinks' and actualises) the objective, unobserved, and largely hidden world which we try to describe in the mathematical terms of quantum physics, a world which in turn causes the world of human perceptions in our minds.

Mind is the ultimate nature of reality, and if so, there is not so much a problem of how minds can arise from matter, but a problem of how and why matter arises from mind. My basic proposal is that the embodiment of finite minds in a developing material world enables such minds to grow alongside one another in creative self-development and growth in understanding and co-operation. Material bodies both express inner mental or spiritual realities, and enable minds to relate to one another in co-operation and mutual help. The physical world is a medium in which minds can access information, grow in understanding, and act creatively together to realise new forms of value. It is created and sustained as such a medium by the supreme Mind, which, as personal in nature, itself participates in the values realised by finite and developing intelligences, and also co-operatively guides such intelligences towards a fuller sharing in the values of its eternal nature, now enriched by the incorporation of finite values into the divine consciousness.

If this is true, there is a purpose for our existence. We ought to seek truth, beauty, and friendship, and we ought to seek them for everyone without exception. These are objective demands, not just personal preferences. And if the cosmos is created by an ultimate mind, there is a hope that such things will be fully realised sometime. This is the foundation of Christian belief in God.

4
Revelation

THIS ARGUMENT MAY have seemed rather abstract, and it may seem far removed from the God of Abraham and Isaac. But it is not. It does not demonstrate that God exists, as if the objective physical world just obviously exists, while God is a sort of extra being who may or may not exist. The whole point is to stand this way of thinking on its head, and see consciousness as the only ultimate reality, with matter as a means of expressing the nature and purposes of mind. God, the ultimate mind, provides a good personal explanation of the cosmos, and gives positive value and purpose to the existence of the cosmos, and to all intelligent lives within the cosmos. Belief in God is not a leap of blind faith; it is the adoption of a highly rational and plausible hypothesis which both explains the existence of the world as we know it, and reveals something of the purpose and value of human life.

However, this is not yet the God of the Christian faith, the Father of Jesus Christ. To get to that, appeal to revelation is needed. What this preliminary idea of God provides is a good reason for taking revelation seriously. If there is such an eternal and necessary, yet also freely creative and responsive, mind of the cosmos, it is reasonable to think that it will provide some idea of its presence, nature, and purpose to intelligent creatures.

I assume that the divine Mind, as good, is concerned with the welfare of all intelligent creatures, not just a few of them. So, I would expect some awareness of the divine Mind in many cultural traditions throughout the world. I also assume that, as in any field of human activity, humans develop their ideas as they learn more about the world and realise more clearly the demands of goodness and the true nature of ultimate values. Given these two assumptions, I would look for a number of developing traditions which may

REVELATION

express different, but not wholly incompatible, perspectives, on the divine Mind, and which each develop (often but not always) towards a deeper understanding of its nature and purpose. Revelation will then take different forms, and will consist in encouraging a development of human understanding from a number of rather different starting-points.

I belong to a Christian tradition of revelation. I am not religiously neutral. But I believe it is very important to place Christian faith in a global context which contains many different claims to revelation, and in a historical context which acknowledges many changes in understanding within any specific faith. I have little sympathy with exclusive views which think that only one religious tradition, or even only one part of that tradition, has the truth, and that other traditions have nothing of value to teach. This denies the universality of God's care for all creatures. I also have little sympathy with an ahistorical view which holds that a particular faith has remained and should always remain unchanged throughout history. A minimal knowledge of the history of any tradition clearly demonstrates that it will have splintered into many different factions and taken many different forms. A medieval Catholic High Mass is very different from Jesus' Last Supper, and doctrines like transubstantiation or Purgatory have a definite, and rather late, date for their first appearance in the tradition. Appeals which are sometimes heard to return to 'the original faith' in fact have to invent that origin for themselves, because no one can go back in time to see what the origin really was.

Diversity and change are features of every religious faith. Each person will have their own set of religious (or non-religious) forms of belief. Understanding of this set will be vastly increased by knowing where it stands in relation to other different understandings, and at what points in history the understanding began to take shape. In my case, for instance, my understanding of Christian revelation has been expanded by seeing East Asian concerns with balance and harmony in nature, Buddhist emphases on compassion for all sentient beings, and Vedantic (Hindu) teaching on the ultimate unity of the self and the divine. These can all be seen as 'revelations' of what I term the divine Mind, as it has been apprehended in love of nature, the way of non-attachment and selflessness, and an apprehension of the ultimate unity of all things in a supreme consciousness.

Naturally, in putting it this way, I am seeing these other traditions from the viewpoint of the Abrahamic tradition, to which I primarily belong. No one can pretend to absolute neutrality, or to having beliefs which are not influenced in many ways by others. It is important to be aware of what these influences are, and to see how they also are parts of constantly developing processes of experience and reflection.

This view I have called 'expansivism'. It is not exclusivist, saying that only my own faith is true. It is not inclusivist, saying that there is truth in other faiths, but only mine is fully true. It is not pluralist, saying that all faiths are more or less equally true. Expansivism is committed in general to one faith, but holds that one can expand (and sometimes correct) one's own faith by insights from other traditions.

The important point is the fact that everyone's beliefs do have a wider global context, and a number of historically dateable origins. To know and learn from that context, and to acknowledge those historical points of origin, is to understand one's own tradition more adequately.

5

Interpreting the Bible

TAKING THE BIBLE, obviously an important part of my primary tradition, as an example, it is a great help to see that the creation stories of Genesis arise in the context of Babylonian and Sumerian creation myths. Many of the features of the Genesis story are explained by that connection. The primeval struggle between Marduk and Tiamat, for instance, becomes the struggle of Jahweh with Leviathan, the chaos monster of the salt-water sea. What the Genesis story does, unlike the Babylonian Genesis, is to assert the existence of one creator God who shapes humans 'in his own image', that is, as potentially capable of sharing in the divine nature. This is a key religious change. When we see that, it helps us to see what sort of story the Genesis account is. It is a myth carrying a spiritual meaning, not a scientific account. And it prepares us for many changes to come, as the biblical history unfolds.

Those changes involve moving from an early view of God as one god, the tribal god of Abraham, among many other gods, to a later view, in the major prophets, of God as the only creator of everything other than Godself. God is at first seen as a rather vengeful figure who destroys almost everyone in a great flood, who kills people who touch the sacred Ark or walk on the sacred mountain, and who in general is pretty dangerous and fearful. But as thought develops, God becomes a being who is merciful as well as just, and who loves the creation and cares for the welfare of all humanity.

If you add the New Testament to the Hebrew Bible, Jesus seems to teach that God is in fact a being of unlimited love (see the Lukan parables of the Good Samaritan and the Prodigal Son), though there are still relics, mostly in Matthew's Gospel, of a rather vindictive belief that the unrighteous will suffer 'eternal punishment' (if that is a correct interpretation of Matthew's phrase in Matthew 25:46, which I doubt). And whereas the God of some classical prophecies simply destroys vast numbers of the wicked,

INTERPRETING THE BIBLE

the God of the New Testament letters to the Colossians and Ephesians promises to unite 'all things in heaven and earth' in Christ (see Ephesians 1:10).

God does not change in these ways. What changes is people's understanding of God, of what justice requires, and of what unlimited love of everyone without exception actually entails. Seen in this light, the Bible becomes a record of the evolving understanding of God which occurred in early Judaism. It is to that tradition that we owe the idea of God as a just and merciful creator, with a good purpose for creation, who makes moral demands on people but also forgives those who sincerely repent.

The Bible is not a textbook, written by God in person, giving a detailed history of the twelve tribes, detailed prophecies of exactly what is going to happen next in history (which unfortunately rarely happened exactly as predicted), lists of commands which are supposed to be clear and changeless (613 of them!), and include some rather dubious rules which include recommendations of polygamy, slavery, the subordination of women, and capital punishment.

The Bible makes much more sense as one of the best records we have of the development of thinking about morality and about God, the spiritual basis of reality, in the history of the Jewish people. The Bible is not a book of rules which must be obeyed in every detail or which has to be taken as absolutely historically accurate.

When we come to the New Testament, we have four accounts of the life and teachings of Jesus, one of which (John) is markedly different from the others; some letters by various people, some of them calling themselves 'Paul'; and a book of cryptic prophecies ('Revelation'). The four Gospels are written in Greek, often rather ungrammatical (especially Mark), and report words of Jesus which were originally spoken in Aramaic. They show all the signs of being edited collections of memories which had been handed down orally by various groups of disciples. The Gospel of John puts into the mouth of Jesus long speeches which

INTERPRETING THE BIBLE

really seem to be theological statements of the belief that he was a human 'incarnation' or embodiment of the eternal 'Logos', the thought or wisdom of God. The letters of Paul, especially Galatians, which most scholars think was by him, stress that what is important for Christians is life 'in the Spirit'. The second letter to the Corinthians says that 'the letter kills, but the Spirit gives life' (3:6). And the letter to the Romans says that Christ is 'the end of the law' (10:4). It is slightly ironic, in view of this, that some Christians take the letter of some of Paul's own opinions as if they were new laws, and have to be believed.

Christian faith focusses on the person of Jesus as a supreme revelation of God. Jesus never wrote a book, however, so it seems most unlikely that he intended to leave a verbally exact record of what God wished to say through him (as Mohammad, for instance, did). Most of what Jesus said and did has not been recorded. We know that he had a reputation as a healer and exorcist, that he had disciples, whom he sent out with the message that the 'kingdom of God' had come near (Mark 1:15), that he was very critical of the religious authorities, and that after a short ministry of about three years he was put to death.

More controversially, he was believed by some, and maybe claimed himself, to be the 'Anointed One' of God (the 'Messiah'), a Davidic King of Israel, whom he called the 'Son of Man', who founded a new community of the divine Spirit, thus fulfilling various biblical prophecies about the renewal and possibly the expansion of God's covenant with Israel. After his death, he was seen by some of his disciples in a series of visionary appearances ('the resurrection'), and he ascended to the presence of God, sending the divine Spirit on the disciples and commissioning them to proclaim a message of the forgiveness of sins through his self-sacrificial death and the promise of eternal life in union with his risen form.

These things are recorded in the Gospels, and they are the only records we have of Jesus, so they are of great importance to Christians. But they are records of the impact Jesus had

INTERPRETING THE BIBLE

on his disciples, and of the new life of hope and joy that he had inspired, and of a sense that the divine Spirit was felt to be at work within them, bringing this new life into being.

There is no reason to think that such records are, or should be, inerrant in every detail. Like the Hebrew Bible, the New Testament is a mixture of different views and memories, some of them not free of elements of prejudice and vindictiveness. I have mentioned that Matthew can be quite vindictive at times. The idea of a Hell from which there can be no escape, which developed quite early in the Christian church, partly because of an unduly literal interpretation of Matthew, has certainly not understood that God is a God of limitless love for all. Teachings about the subordination of women to men have certainly not understood that in Christ there is 'neither male nor female' (Galatians 3:28). Fantastic expectations of Armageddon and the Last Judgment still portray God as a vindictive and violent judge.

It is, in my view, of the utmost importance that Christians should be aware of the ambiguity of all religion, and of Christianity in particular. There are exclusivist interpretations of Christianity (if you do not explicitly believe in Jesus you cannot be saved); there are vindictive elements in Christianity (if you do not behave you will go to Hell for ever); and there are moments of violent intolerance in Christianity (Christ will return and inflict vengeance on all who do not believe in God – 2 Thessalonians 1:7 and 8).

The only rational and morally acceptable way to deal with this is to appeal to human ignorance and hatred, and admit that it will exist in any organisation, including religious ones. If the Bible is seen as a record of the views of humans, it will not be free of such elements. But it is our only set of testimonies to how fallible men and women saw a new vision of God in the person of Jesus, a vision which gave them a new sense of value and purpose in life. That is its importance – it is a first-hand witness to the new life and understanding of God which Jesus brought.

6
The Kingdom of God

CHRISTIAN FAITH IS absolutely monotheistic. There is only one creator God; there is only one mind and will in God; and God's ultimate purpose for the cosmos is that all things will share in the divine nature (2 Peter 1:4). Many things within the cosmos will be signs, revelations, of these truths. The Jewish tradition, through its prophets, developed the idea of one personal creator, and the *Torah* taught that Jews were called by God to be 'a priestly kingdom' (Exodus 19:6), to imitate in their own lives the goodness and compassion of God and to be witnesses to the divine call and promise, which were for the whole world. Jewish law, the *Torah*, tried to articulate the moral demands of God and to express the ideal life of loving friendship with the divine, a covenant of love.

Jesus was a Jew who, his disciples

believed, realised the moral demands of God fully in his own life, and thus brought the 'kingdom of God', the rule of God, near, indeed, making it present in his own person. His disciples believed that he had a supremely intimate and intense knowledge and love of God, and that God worked in and through him to heal, to forgive, and to bring new hope and joy to those who followed him. He was seen as an embodiment, an 'incarnation', of divine wisdom and love, and revered as the 'Christ' (Greek for 'Messiah'), the anointed King of the line of David, who would liberate his people from tyranny and oppression, and bring '*shalom*', peace and fulfilment to his people.

His kingdom, however, was not a political kingdom. It is, as it was in him, the rule of the divine Spirit in the hearts of men and women. The liberation he brings is from pride, greed, and hatred; the kingdom he rules is a kingdom of the heart, whose fruits are 'love, joy, peace, patience, kindness, generosity, faithfulness, gentleness, and self-control' (Galatians 5:22).

I think of the kingdom of God as threefold

in nature: an earthly kingdom, a heavenly kingdom, and an eternal kingdom. The person of the historical Jesus embodies in his own person the rule of God, the earthly kingdom. He mediates to his disciples the divine Spirit that filled his life, so that they too can know God in a more intimate way and share in the power of God to heal and forgive. Their lives are to be patterned on his, and to be empowered by the Spirit that they receive from him. This is to be a new community, a covenant of love for the whole world, ruled not by written laws but by the power of God's love working within them. Being composed of ordinary men and women, it will be a flawed and often failing community. But it nevertheless is called and empowered to mediate the love of God which was in Jesus Christ to the world.

I would say two things about this earthly kingdom, which is of course the church in all its varied forms. First, it is not a political kingdom and the goal of earthly power and dominance is completely opposed to all its ideals. It is not a community of those who are 'saved'; it is a community which exists to mediate the love of God to others. If it is an 'elect', chosen by God, the choice is of those who are to serve selflessly, not of those who form some sort of spiritual elite.

Second, this 'new covenant' does not replace the first covenant with the Jewish people, which will never be rejected by God. It is a major tragedy that there was ever a major split with Judaism, and shameful that Christians have often persecuted Jews. Christians should thank God that they follow a Jew who is their King, and who widens God's covenant to include them as members.

7

The World to Come

THAT IS THE FIRST form of the Kingdom, the earthly kingdom. The second form, the heavenly kingdom, is pictured in the New Testament, in what is obviously symbol or metaphor, as a great feast in the world to come, after physical death, with Abraham and the prophets, but also people drawn from the whole Gentile world (Matthew 8:11). In it are all those who have truly loved God, whether soon or late.

Christians believe in life after physical death. Partly this is because Jesus appeared to the disciples after his physical death. Partly it is because a truly good God would not leave the suffering of millions of lives without any remedy or point, but would be able, in a larger form of existence, to give meaning to all earthly lives and bring them to fulfilment and happiness.

A philosophical idealist has no problems with the continuation of consciousness after death, for consciousness does not essentially depend on a link with some specific physical body. A body is what enables people to express their thoughts publicly, to identify one another and to act in a common world. It is therefore natural for a consciousness to have some form of body. But there can be many forms of body, and in 1 Corinthians 15, Paul writes that the physical body (*soma psychikon*) is different from the spiritual body (*soma pneumatikon*). We die as physical bodies, in a world controlled by the law of entropy or decay. We continue to exist as spiritual bodies, in a different sort of world, not subject to decay. The world to come is not in this spacetime, but it is a world where individual and social life can exist.

Paul's account fits well with the reports of Jesus' resurrection, which are brief appearances of a body behind locked doors, or unrecognised for long walks, and which disappears as suddenly as it appears. Jesus, like all humans, continued to exist as a spiritual body, after his physical death on the cross. According to 1 Peter, chapters 3 and 4, in the world of the dead he preached so

THE WORLD TO COME

that people who had died like all men, including those who were very wicked, would have the chance to live in the Spirit. In some way, those in the world to come are conscious and active.

According to the parable of Lazarus (Luke 16:19-31) there are two divisions of the world to come. One is 'Abraham's bosom', where the just or penitent exist – this is Paradise, or the heavenly kingdom. The other is described as a world of fire. Other metaphors for this are a fiery furnace, an outer darkness, a prison, and a place of anguish and the 'gnashing of teeth' (mostly in Matthew). This would be a place in which those who had been unloving and cruel on earth would experience for themselves the harm they had done, and would learn what it is like to be shut out by their own actions from love and joy.

A crucial feature of the Gospels is Jesus' teaching that he came to find those who were lost in hatred and greed (in 'sin') and invite them to turn again to the God who always wished for their liberation and fulfilment. The parable of the Prodigal Son teaches that anyone who wishes, if only after long and bitter experience, to turn from hatred to love, will be met with joy by God, who will empower them to do so. There is judgment on those who have caused immense harm and frustrated the purposes of God. There is punishment, though that is not a set penalty imposed by God, whatever the consequences for them. If God is indeed good, punishment will be corrective, intended to bring them to turn back from evil and accept the liberating power of the Spirit. And punishment will be self-imposed, not torture by God (no loving God could torture anyone), but the regret and bitterness of finding themselves in the company of those who are filled with hate and greed, now exposed in its full destructive power, and shut out from joy and true friendship.

The Gospel is that God desires that all should be united to the divine in wisdom and love (1 Timothy 2:4). The sadness of what has come to be called 'Hell' (not a biblical word) is both self-imposed, and intended to lead to true repentance. Hope is never lost, even in Hell, for the love of God in Christ can never be defeated even by the deepest Hell of misery and hatred

(Romans 8:38 and 39). If the Gospel is true, Hell is not everlasting.

This does not mean that all will be liberated, for human freedom may resist to the end, however irrational that is. But there will be an end, when all evil, including Hell itself, is destroyed, and everything that remains, everything in heaven and earth, is finally united in Christ.

Presumably Jesus, though in some form he appeared in 'Hades', the world of the dead, after the death of his physical body, truly existed in the heavenly kingdom. This heavenly form of Jesus is quite different from his physical form, and we cannot know what it is like (1 John 3:2). When Jesus appeared to the disciples, this was a series of relatively brief earthly appearances of what was already a spiritual body in a different realm of being.

It follows that the resurrection was not a breaking of all the laws of physics. What was unusual about it was the transfiguration of his physical body into a spiritual body (leaving the tomb empty), and the appearances in this spacetime of a body which already existed in a different realm of being, which is certainly not impossible if there are spiritual realities beyond this world. It is even probable, if God wished to show that life endures beyond the grave, and that Jesus was the human person through whom God's purpose of uniting humans to the divine life was to be accomplished.

All descriptions of Jesus' heavenly existence and his 'visit' to Hades are highly metaphorical, not literal descriptions, and the realities are virtually impossible to imagine. But it is important to see that the Jesus whose image we see in many churches is not the historical Jesus. We have no idea what he looked like, and presumably his knowledge was limited to what people of his time could have known, with the addition of his exceptional acquaintance with God. The images we see are constructions of our imagination, symbols comprehensible to us, of what we cannot yet see as he truly is, the heavenly Christ, whose knowledge is no longer that of a young Jewish man, though his transfigured humanity still functions as a mediator of the divine to us, an 'image of the invisible God'.

8

The Incarnation

THERE IS ALSO a third aspect of the Christ. It is the Christ as the eternal Word of God, through whom all things were created and in whom all things will be united (Colossians 1:16 and Ephesians 1:10). This form of Christ is not the young human person who expressed the rule of God in his life in Israel. It is not the transfigured human person who 'sits at the right hand of the Father' – that is, who, existing in a spiritual realm of being, mediates the power and love of God to the human world. It is an eternal and uncreated aspect of God, an all-embracing spiritual reality which is to liberate and fulfil all creation, even, according to the letter to the Ephesians, to include all creation within itself.

The eternal Christ, according to John's Gospel, 'became flesh' (John 1:14). I interpret this to mean that the Eternal Word was expressed or manifested in the historical person of Jesus.

I accept the traditional formula of the Council of Chalcedon, in 451AD, that Jesus was fully human, but also fully divine, that he was 'two natures in one person'. But those technical terms, 'nature' and 'person', derive from ancient Greek philosophical thought, and they can be rather misleading to people today. In Aristotelian-influenced medieval Latin Christianity, they become especially perplexing. That is because the divine nature, assumed to be perfect, is taken to be simple (containing no complexity), immutable (not capable of any change), and impassible (not capable of suffering). Human nature, on the other hand, is essentially complex, changeable and capable of suffering and happiness. It is then very difficult to see how those natures, so defined, can co-exist. And if a 'person' is taken to be the subject of a rational consciousness, it is difficult to see how there can be only one such subject of two completely different natures.

THE INCARNATION

Personal Idealists, like me, do not have these difficulties. The divine nature is mind, and thinks, feels, and acts in new creative ways. In fact, creative change and responsive relationship to other (presumably created) minds seem essential possibilities of a supreme mind. Creativity and loving relationship are properties which it is better to have than to lack, so God will possess them, and be complex, capable of creative change, and of feeling both happiness and sadness. God will be a subject of consciousness, one which is dimensionally greater than any finite subject of consciousness. God is much more than that, but of that 'more' we cannot speak, and it remains true that, while God is not really 'a person', we can truly speak of God as personal mind, while insisting that there is much more of God that our minds cannot comprehend.

Jesus, as fully human, will possess a finite subject of consciousness. In this way, there will be two subjects of mind and will, one uncreated and divine and one finite and human, united in Jesus. What sort of unity could this be?

I suspect that some finite expression of the personal aspect of the divine is essential to the divine nature, if the divine nature is essentially creatively free and capable of responsive relationships of love and compassion. A finite cosmos will be a creative expression of God, and finite created minds will make it possible for God to have new forms of experience and to act in new ways. For God will know 'from inside', as it were, the experiences of finite minds, which will involve suffering as well as happiness. And God will be able to act through and in co-operation with finite agents, in ways which could not exist without a created world.

The cosmos is thus a direct expression of divine creativity and a realisation of possibilities inherent in the divine nature. The cosmos as a whole is destined to be an embodiment or 'incarnation' of the divine, though of course it is incapable of fully expressing all that is in the uncreated divine nature.

THE INCARNATION

The incarnation of relevant aspects of the divine nature in a human individual is on this view a natural extension of creation, not something which somehow interrupts the normal processes of nature. The human mind of Jesus contributes to the experiences of God, and mediates aspects of divine wisdom and creative power in the world. The human mind retains its own unique experiences, though God knows what they are, and it retains its own creative power, though God supplements that power by influencing and co-operating with it.

A human mind could have access to the divine mind by direct unmediated acquaintance with the contents of the divine mind. This would not mean that the human mind was omniscient, knowing all possible worlds, for example. Such a thing could not be contained in any finite mind. But it could be aware of the divine presence in an immediate way, be filled with a love of supreme goodness, and discern at least the general purposes of the divine.

The divine mind would experience all the feelings of every finite mind. But finite minds are endowed with creative freedom, and they could make choices which lead them away from God, and they could possess self-interested attachments which lead them to acts conflicting with the divine purpose. If they did, God would 'stand apart' from them, preserving their freedom, but only assuming into the divine mind feelings which have been purged of evil, and distancing itself from all evil and ambiguous feelings. In the case of Jesus, God is postulated to have created a human mind which was without the 'inclination to sin', without egoism, hatred, and greed. The experiences of Jesus could therefore be assumed directly into God, without any estrangement or alienation.

Human minds have creative freedom to act, but they can choose positive values or destructive practices, and in virtually all human cases they do. This means that the divine mind could only seek to frustrate their choices, and ensure that they do not finally succeed. But if there was someone who always chose positive and creative values, God could co-operate

THE INCARNATION

to increase their wisdom and creative power, giving them extraordinary gifts which perhaps should have been present in everyone, and perhaps will be again, in the 'new creation' which will follow on the death of this cosmos.

Christians generally believe that Jesus was such a one. He had extraordinary knowledge and love of God, and extraordinary gifts of insight and healing. He was a human person united to the divine mind in such a way that in him divine and human were co-operatively united in the closest possible way, two minds in an unbreakable union, in such a way that he could say, 'The Father [God] and I are one' (John 10:30). A finite mind, though possessing its own creativity and experience, became the human incarnation of the uncreated divine mind, the 'Word made flesh'.

9
The Atonement

THE THIRD AND final form of the kingdom of God is the liberation of creation from all estrangement from God, and the fulfilment of the divine goal of creation.

The creative choices by humans on our planet have largely been made to favour short-term self-interest and ruthless competition for survival. Over many generations, our world has become estranged and alienated from the cosmic mind and purpose which is its basis. It has become a place of pride, hatred, and greed. That is what the creation myths of Genesis describe, though they necessarily used the primitive ideas about the Universe that were then held.

As a Christian, I believe that God created a human life in this estranged world that was uniquely and fully united to the divine life. The Word (*logos*) of God is that aspect of the divine being which unites a human life to itself, making that life an image of the divine nature and the initiator of a way to reconcile estranged humanity to the divine.

This initiation is known traditionally as 'the Atonement', the making one of God and all humanity and its liberation from pride, greed, and hatred. It is only God who has the power to bring about this liberation and union. But the divine, in its aspect as the eternal Christ, does so on this planet in and through the human Jesus. His life shows what love is. His death shows that God shares in the sufferings of estranged humans, and goes to the furthest possible lengths to bring them back to God. His whole life was a sacrifice of self to the divine, culminating in the ultimate sacrifice of the cross. His transfiguration into glory in the resurrection life shows that the power of love cannot be overcome by death. And the continued presence of the Spirit which filled his life in the hearts of men and women begins the process of reconciliation by which all can be finally united to God.

THE ATONEMENT

The New Testament suggests a number of different images of the atonement, but for me the image of Jesus taking a punishment in my place, which has been quite widespread, while being emotionally effective, implies a rather harsh view of punishment as purely retributive, not corrective, as well as seeming to accept the view that it is morally acceptable for an innocent person to be punished in place of a guilty one. I am uncomfortable with these implications. I would wish to stress that it is God who suffers on the cross, not just the human Jesus. And that is a sign that God shares in all the suffering of creation, but that self-giving divine love ensures that joy and fulfilment is God's will for all sentient beings.

Such joy and fulfilment will come when all creation is united 'in Christ'. The eternal Word was united to the human person of Jesus, so making them one. The destiny God wills for all humans is that the eternal Word should unite them within its supra-cosmic spiritual reality.

All will know and love God fully, and all will co-operate with God to work out new creative purposes of intrinsic worth. All will be parts of the one divine life, free from alienation and destructive conflict, unfolded in innumerable different forms.

10

The Trinity and the Redemption of the Cosmos

TODAY WE KNOW that the cosmos is immensely older and vaster than anyone imagined in Jesus' day. Then it was thought that earth was the centre of a set of concentric spheres on which sun, moon, and stars, envisaged as small lights, were placed, with heaven just beyond the outermost sphere. The whole universe was only a few thousand years old, and it would probably not last much longer.

Now we know that there are billions of galaxies, other suns, and planets capable of producing life; that the cosmos began billions of years ago, and will last for billions of years more, before it finally runs out of energy. From a primal 'Big Bang', integrated and complex life-forms with consciousness have evolved, and the process of evolution is continuing.

This changes our whole theological perspective. As a personal Idealist, I see

God as the cosmic spiritual generator and sustainer of this evolutionary process. From a primal simple and unconscious 'void' the cosmos is shaped by a supreme intelligence to generate communities of finite, conscious, and freely creative minds, perhaps on many planets, of which our earth is only one.

The process of cosmic evolution is governed by laws which are, in an almost incredible way, precisely fitted to produce carbon-based life-forms. These laws are regular enough to be understandable and usable by such life-forms, and 'loose' enough to allow creative choices to be made. Regularity, chance, and creative choice, all have a place in the cosmic process.

In modern cosmology, we know that humans are almost certainly only one small part of intelligent life within the cosmos. God the creator will be concerned for the cosmos as a whole, not just with this small planet. It is to be expected that the eternal Christ will take many forms on many worlds. The human person of Jesus is perhaps one among many finite images of the Word of God, a Word which in its full spiritual reality surpasses anything we can imagine. Jesus is Christ for us. But the cosmic Christ is that in which the whole creation holds together, and in which the whole creation, not just human beings, will be united.

The New Testament speaks of the *Parousia*, the 'return' or the 'presence' of Jesus. In Christian liturgies, we say that 'Christ will come again'. In the old and outdated Biblical cosmology, this might have been interpreted literally. It would never be quite literal, since the talk of Jesus coming on clouds, trumpets blowing, and people rising into the air, is hardly to be taken literally; it uses the poetic symbolism common among the prophets of Israel. But many early Christians did think the world might end quite soon.

Modern cosmology calls for a complete revision of such beliefs. Whatever happens to the earth, the whole creation will not end for billions of years. The Genesis myth says that all things come from God, but is not a historical account of what happened not very long ago in the past. In a similar way, the 'end of time' myths just say that all things will return to God, and that Christ will appear to all as the eternal Word who was in Jesus, finally completing the goal of creation, but they are not literal predictions about what will happen in the near future.

This realisation helps to explain the much misunderstood verse, 'I am the way ... no one comes to the Father but by me' (John 14:6). As in much of John's Gospel, the 'I' here refers to the eternal Word, who is one with Jesus, but is a cosmic spiritual reality not confined to the person of Jesus. No one comes to God except by way of the Wisdom of God, which, on this planet, is visibly expressed in the person of Jesus. It does not mean that you have to believe in Jesus to enter into final communion of being with God, an interpretation that is clearly absurd if there are life-forms in other galaxies which God cares about.

The Word or wisdom of God, the eternal Christ, simply is God, in a distinctive mode of personal being which unites with finite lives to unite them to the divine. God, being complex, may have many modes of being. Three of them are described in Christian faith as a 'Trinity' of Father, Son, and Spirit. They are the three major ways in which God is, in relation to human beings. The 'Son' is God united to Jesus on this planet ('son', in the tradition, means 'one chosen by God', not a physically generated child). The 'Father' is God in Godself, transcendently existing beyond the cosmos as its origin and sustainer (regarded by Jesus as 'Father', as a spiritual reality with personal qualities, who is the source of Jesus' being). The 'Spirit' is God being present and acting in human hearts and minds. There is just one mind and will in God, but these are three aspects or forms in which Christians see God as existing and acting in relation to humans, and in analogous but unknown ways throughout the whole creation.

The doctrine of the Trinity has been complicated in Christian tradition by the Aristotelian idea that God is simple, timeless, and changeless. This does not fit well with the idea that there are least three ways of being in the same God. A different, more recent, idea is that there are three 'persons', three distinct subjects of mind and will, who relate to one another in love, and together form God. This is, to my mind, too near to polytheism to be acceptable. It does express the insight that 'God is love' (1 John 4:8), so that it is a divine perfection to relate to others in love. But it tries to regard these 'others' as other omnipotent and omniscient and uncreated beings, and as parts of one eternal God, whereas what 'otherness' really requires is that the others really are different from God, that is, that they are creatures. It seems to me more consistent with the unlimited love of God to see God as essentially related in love, not just to two others within the divine being, but to every created mind.

All created persons are, or when reconciled will be, parts of God (will be 'in Christ'). They are nevertheless not divine, not maximally powerful or knowing. They are created, and have their own unique experiences and creative powers. Yet they share in the divine nature, and in it they find their liberation and fulfilment.

For this reason, I think the traditional phrase, 'The Trinity is three persons in one substance', is better reformulated in some such way as, 'The Trinity is three aspects or modes of being of the one personal reality which is God', as both the Catholic theologian Karl Rahner and the Protestant theologian Karl Barth, have suggested.

The Trinitarian God - transcendent, finitely expressed in Jesus, and present within all created persons throughout the universe - is the Christian vision of the supreme mind of the cosmos, who calls all creation out of estrangement and suffering into a joyful communion of love. As the New Testament puts it: 'God was in Christ, reconciling the world [and I think we need to make clear that, with our expanded knowledge of the universe, this means the whole cosmos] to himself' (1 Corinthians 5:19).

Appendix

Recent books by the author relevant to the following chapters:

1 – 3: *More Than Matter* (Lion Hudson, 2010), and *The Christian Idea of God* (CUP, 2017) and *The Evidence for God* (DLT, 2014)
4: *Religion in the Modern World* (CUP, 2019)
5: *What the Bible Really Teaches* (SPCK, 2004)
6 – 9: *Sharing in the Divine Nature* (Wipf and Stock, 2020) and *Parables of Time and Eternity* (Wipf and Stock, 2021)
10: *Christ and the Cosmos* (CUP, 2015)

MY THEOLOGY

The world's leading Christian thinkers explain some of the principal tenets of their theological beliefs.

Collect the full library.

September 2021

1. Robert Beckford
2. Ilia Delio
3. Malcolm Guite
4. Alister McGrath

November 2021

5. Guy Consolmagno
6. Ann Loades
7. Rachel Mann
8. Keith Ward

January 2022

9. Cynthia Bourgeault
10. Grace Ji-Sun Kim
11. John Swinton
12. Mpho Tutu van Furth

March 2022

13. Joan Chittister
14. Scot McKnight
15. Siku